First published in 2000 by
PERETTI PUBLISHING,
Devon, England.

Front cover photograph by John G. Murray,
by kind permission of John Murray Publishers Ltd.

Back cover photograph by kind permission of Jonathan Stedall

William Rushton's cartoon of John Betjeman appears by kind
permission of Mr. Toby Rushton

British Library Cataloguing in Publication Data
A Catalogue record of this book is available from the British Library
'Still Sidmouth'
Betjeman, John

ISBN 0 906038 09 X

Book design by Joe Pieczenko at Newton St. Cyres, Devon

The publication of 'Still Sidmouth' has been made possible
by the enlightened generosity of

SOUTH WEST WATER LIMITED

A Pennon Group Plc Company

Still Sidmouth

John Betjeman

Poet Laureate, 1972 - 1984

peretti

PERETTI PUBLISHING

"Leisure to live and breathe and smell and look, Unfold for me this seaside history book."

We are indebted to many people for their encouragement, kindness and generosity in helping us bring Sir John Betjeman's 'lost' poem of 'Sidmouth' to book. It is a small poem but it is an important one. Uniquely for the man who was to become Britain's poet laureate, it was written as the commentary to what used to be called a 'documentary' film. Like its subject, the English seaside town of Sidmouth, in Devon, it has great charm and the words and images capture a fleeting glance of a world which, in the summer of 1962 was already changing fast.

It was also one of the first films which Jonathan Stedall made and it marked the beginning of a lifelong friendship between the two men.

But we should like to begin our thanks where we first began, with Gerry Dawson, an independent film producer at his Blue Pyjamas Productions, for pointing us in several right directions, simultaneously. Gerry was at HTV in Bristol in 1993 when he found a dusty pile of tins of 16mm film. He had 're-discovered' the series of John Betjeman television films made by Jonathan Stedall for TWW in the early 1960s. The material was in a state of neglect and the film 'Sidmouth' was even missing its original soundtrack. After extensive restoration it was recorded again by Nigel Hawthorne, who brought his own inspired interpretation to the text. Gerry Dawson was the Series Editor of the restored programmes, finally transmitted by Channel 4 as 'The Lost Betjemans' in 1994, a full generation after they had last been shown. He writes, "It is a delight to see these things come to life again after nearly 40 years. The films are lovely but a book is a firm, tangible, treasure that can be dipped into time and again to provide a souvenir, a memory, for those who love Sidmouth."

The small images that here accompany the text have been taken from the HTV master tape and we thank the company for its generosity in allowing us to use them. We must particularly thank Jeremy Payne for making that possible – and Mirinda Rowell and Mark Renwick for bringing about, first the formalities and then the technicalities of the electronic transfers.

Jonathan Stedall was the director of the original series of films. He most generously took time off from his own writing and film work to compose the Introduction which follows. It provides the backdrop and sets the scene at Sidmouth in the early 1960s. Each of his films is a work of art as well as a small celebration of the life of the West Country. That they were also "tremendous fun" to make was the clue which led us to the door of Sir John's publisher, John Murray, Publishers, London, when we were in search of an image for our front cover. Our thanks to Mr. John R. Murray for allowing us to reproduce this wonderful photograph, taken by his father, Mr. "Jock" Murray, of Sir John, "proof reading."

The picture of Sidmouth on the poem's opening page was the opening shot in the original film and we are indebted to the owners of the print, Messrs Peter Eley, estate agents in Sidmouth, for allowing us to use the image and for proving to be such a mine of information about their town.

In spite of the increase in traffic since the film was made, Sidmouth remains 'Still Sidmouth' – England's most cherished seaside town!

John and Margaret Fisher
PERETTI PUBLISHING, Devon

THE BETJEMAN SOCIETY

From Lady Wilson of Rievaulx
President of the Betjeman Society

I am so glad that this poem, "Sidmouth" is to be reproduced as a booklet – it is a delightful poem, in Sir John's particular style, full of detail – how he loved small details – and beautifully descriptive of the town.

It is such a pleasure to read a poem which rhymes and scans!

I am sure that this little book will be a great success and, gentle reader, I heartily commend it to you!

Mary Wilson.

The making of *Sidmouth* with John Betjeman

I was 23 years old when I first met and worked with John Betjeman. I had just started as a young director for TWW in Cardiff and Bristol (now HTV) and these were to be my first films. Our brief was to create portraits of places in the West Country that were close to Betjeman's heart. Over two years

Jonathan Stedall

we filmed at Sidmouth, Clevedon, Sherborne, Marlborough, Bath, Swindon, Crewkerne, Devizes, Weston-super-Mare and Malmesbury. Sidmouth was, I believe, the first place we visited together.

At each location we would spend two or three days planning the programme. I would then return with a cameraman (and occasionally a sound-recordist) for a couple of days of filming. These were modest productions, yet made with great care and love by all those involved. Essentially the films worked and still have a certain appeal, I believe, because we were trusted and left alone. We were free to be spontaneously creative at every stage of the production. Above all I remember it as tremendous fun!

Betjeman himself was undoubtedly a genius. His enthusiasm, knowledge and imagination were a constant inspiration. He knew a great deal about architecture and social history, but he was also fascinated by the here and now. Who lived in those buildings today?

Were they troubled or happy? What did they eat for breakfast? People interested Betjeman above all else, and for this reason he enjoyed immensely the teamwork that making a film demands.

One incident at Sidmouth I remember with particular amusement. I had previously been working for six months in France for ATV, and there had developed a liking for port. And in France port is drunk as an aperitif. I didn't have a particularly sophisticated background myself. At home my mother had drunk cocoa not port, and after supper not dinner! In our

search for local history Betjeman and I visited a Mr. Silverman who lived in a grand house above the town. It was six o'clock in the evening. We were offered drinks. Without blinking an eye I asked for port. And without blinking an eye Mr. Silverman

gave me one. Only John Betjeman laughed, and he went on doing so for years. In fact I believe he is laughing still!

One of Betjeman's outdstanding qualities was his kindness and I think this shows in the script he wrote for our film about Sidmouth. He did, incidentally, always write his commentaries in the cutting-room once the film was edited. In other words he liked to respond to the images on the screen and had a strong sense of when those images spoke for themselves and needed no words. A lot of his observations are very personal, both in the film about Sidmouth as well as in many others. He imagines, for example, what people might be saying to one another or what they might be thinking. But he is never cruel. True, like all of us he had his bêtes-noires. Developers, greedy farmers and young executives with loud voices are given a hard time in many of his poems. But fundamentally he loved life and people. The films we made together over the years were above all attempts to celebrate the wonderfully comic, touching and poignant moments that permeate all our lives. And it was a privilege indeed to have been a little part of John Betjeman's life.

JONATHAN STEDALL

Still
Sidmouth

by John Betjeman

Thus Sidmouth looked a hundred years ago,
Still much the same it lies these hills below,

Still the old church tower rises in the trees,
But this quaint house's windows, what are these?

They're bits of church, saved from extermination,
By the Victorian's so-called 'restoration.'

Still in the shadow of the tower repose,
'neath handsome Georgian headstones, bones of those

Who built their mansions in this countryside,
Who came for health, bathed quietly here – and died.

Pause at this altar tomb where you can see,
Sculptured, the name of Mister Edward Lee.

And there's his house in 1823

And here it is today. The change is small,
Since George the third was monarch of us all.

Mansions for admirals by the pebbly strand
And cottages for maiden aunts, inland,
That go with tea and strawberries and cream,
Sweet sheltered gardens by the twisting stream,
Cobb, thatch and fuschia bells, a Devon dream.

Yon Gothic castle is the Royal Glen.
Princess Victoria, a baby then
Played with her mother in this garden green
And Sidmouth nurtured England's future Queen.

Why am I talking to this film in rhyme?
It suits the film, it suits the sunny clime,
It rolls with leisured ease these streets along,

It does to this verandah'd world belong.

Gothic or Classic, terrace or hotel,
Here does the backbone of Old England dwell.

Men who have served this country all their lives,
Mothers who smile to see their daughters – wives!

From yonder balcony what eyes look down,
On some young lover strolling in the town?
And from this road what eyes have looked above,
To yon bay window with this light of love?

Here with what happiness could I return,
And watch my own flame dying,
Love's young fire.

See when the sun is at its noon-day height,
Regency ironwork, elegant and light,
It stands out grim against the stucco's white.

Broad crescents basking in the summer sun,
A sense of sea and holidays begun,

Leisure to live and breathe and smell and look,
Unfold for me this seaside history book.

And when the architecture grows more slack,
Among the little houses at the back,
Stucco recedes, Victorian bricks appear,

In Alma Terrace, shades of the Crimea!

Lunchtime is over, now the hour for rest
And snores are gentle as the sun moves West.
In summer silence bricks and blossoms swoon,

All on the drowsy Sidmouth afternoon.

Clocks in a hundred houses chime three,
It's time to saunter to the town for tea.
To exercise the dog and have a chat
On this and this and that and that.

"Two and eleven? My goodness, what a price!
Now don't go there, dear, do take my advice."

"Oh, everything is dearer now I fear,
Do you find dear things so much dearer, dear?"

"Well I, you know, must think before I buy,
My pension's tiny and my rent is high.

Now wait two minutes, dear, wait to shop
At Holmes here, and buy myself a chop.

You don't mind waiting? Well then, watch the meat,
I won't take long my purchase to complete.

Or go to Sellek's, just across the street,
I'll meet you there, I want to buy some paint.

I love these Sidmouth shopping streets –
so quaint."

"Oh, I must tell you, dear, you used to know
That corner cupboard where I like to show
My old Crown Derby? Well it had to go."

Ah, times must change and Sidmouth changes too,
If they did not what would antique shops do?

"Since I have had to hold my purse strings tight,
Shop window gazing is my chief delight.

Look, there's a real feature of the place,
That dear old shop which sells the Devon lace.

That dear old lady there is quite the same,
I'm getting old too – I forget her name.

It's time that I was going home to tea,
Come to the front, come dear with me."

"I'd simply love to – there's a glimpse of sea!"

And on the front, as Sidmouth tea-time ends,
There's always such a chance of meeting friends.

"Uncle! and Auntie Gladys, what a treat!"
"So this is Terence, doesn't he look sweet?
Well, weren't us lucky, all of us to meet?"

As the waves thunder on the shingle shore,

"The wife and I lie back and have a snore."

As the waves thunder on the shingle shore
I like to hear this pebbly backwash roar.
And I lift my eyes to see the sunlight –
Those Georgian cottages with roofs of thatch.

I like to stand upon the Esplanade and look,
Across to where some earthquake moved,
millions of years ago,

Those cliffs of red, bay beyond bay
From sandstone head to head.

Then to watch cricket on the fairest ground,
That ring which exists all England round,
And although cricket bores me, here I find
The pleasant scenery, I ease my mind.

Sun-smitten terrace, sound of ball on bat,
And in the quiet the sudden cry, "How's that!"
The keen sea air so keeps my brain awake,
That even I can some interest take.

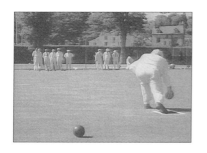 

And if on cricket I would turn my back,
To watch the wood go rolling to the jack,
Well, here's the game that Devon used to play
On Plymouth Hoe, four hundred years away.

Sunset and Sidmouth, sad, I say farewell,
To your warm shallow vale where I would dwell,
Beyond that red, Edwardian hotel.

Pause on Peak Hill, look eastward to the town,
Then to the Connaught Gardens wander down
And in the shelter of its tropic bowers,
I see its bright and outsize Devon flowers.

Farewell, seductive Sidmouth by the sea,
Older and more exclusive than Torquay,

Sidmouth in Devon; you're the town for me!

John Betjeman

The End

1968
TWW's final transmission

Post Script

JOHN BETJEMAN, to camera,
at TWW's final transmission, 1968.

"Now TWW or Telly Welly as I call it, was a good firm to work for. Telly Welly wanted me to make some films of Welsh and West Country towns and they found for me a young producer – Jonathan Stedall, who'd just started with them. We liked the same jokes and we had the same point of view and we worked out our programmes unhampered by accountants and officialdom. Telly Welly, you had a warm, friendly personality. Like many others, I'm very grateful to you. I'm sorry to see you go. It's like the death of an old friend."

JOHN BETJEMAN, in a letter to friend and writer
Terence de Vere White, 1st November, 1967*

"I don't think Television is anything but a minor art – except now and then when immediacy, as at Churchill's funeral, gives it an extra dimension – but I think it is delightful teamwork. And so is filming and the key person is the editor (provided the material to edit is good) and film is an art. It can be the poetry of today."

* "John Betjeman: Letters 1951 – 1984" edited and introduced by Candida Lycett Green.
Extract reproduced by permission of the publishers, Random House Group Ltd.

1962
Camera
GRAHAM EDGAR

Editor
COLIN VOISEY

1962
Producer
JIM DOUGLAS-HENRY

Director
JONATHAN STEDALL